I0711303

Life Skills Workbook & Journal

Volume 1 Wise Mind

Linda Houts, MSW, LCSW

Life Skills Workbook & Journal

Volume 1 Wise Mind

This publication is designed to provide accurate and authoritative information concerning the subject matter covered for educational purposes. It is sold with the understanding that the publisher is not engaged in rendering psychological, financial, legal, or other professional service. If you have questions or concerns about your emotional, psychological, or medical well-being, seek expert assistance of a competent mental health or medical professional.

The views expressed in this work are solely those of the author. Reproduction for client use is authorized. Any other reproduction in any form is prohibited without the express written permission of the author.

Distributed by Amazon Kindle Direct Publishing

Copyright © 2020 by Linda Houts.

Copyright © 2024 by Linda Houts.

All Rights Reserved.

ISBN: 9798655111806

Imprint: Independently published

Contents

Introduction

This workbook is packed with skills and prompts designed to foster introspection, personal growth, and valuable insights. You can use it in several ways: work through it from start to finish, focus on specific topics, or incorporate it as a supplementary resource for therapy or homework.

Each page is crafted to encourage note-taking, highlighting, doodling, and even coloring—whatever helps you engage and reflect.

Enjoy Your Journaling Journey.

1 Dialectics

Dialectics is the skill of cognitive flexibility. By enhancing this flexibility, we improve our ability to think clearly, take different perspectives, practice radical acceptance, remain nonreactive, and enhance emotional functioning, regardless of circumstances or urges.

Dialectics involves recognizing that opposites often coexist in life. The term "dialectical" refers to the idea that two seemingly opposing concepts can both be true simultaneously. In Dialectical Behavior Therapy (DBT), there is always more than one way to think about, view, or feel in any given situation. The more dialectical your thinking, the more flexible it becomes. Increased cognitive flexibility makes it easier to experience emotions in ways that are beneficial to you.

Consider what you are reactive to. What stirs strong emotional responses in you? In what ways is your thinking rigid, upsetting, ruminative, worrisome, black-and-white, all-or-nothing, me vs. them, winning and losing, extreme, fault-finding, or blaming? How might these patterns be off-putting to quality relationships with others or interfere with your life goals?

Dialectics and Socratic Questioning

Dialectics and Socratic questioning are closely related. Dialectics is the process of investigating how "both-and" can be true, rather than "either-or" or "one-or-the-other." It involves exploring the supposed contradiction of seemingly opposing forces at work in the world. The idea that these forces are opposing is an illusion of emotional nearsightedness. Dialectical thinking acknowledges and examines seeming opposites, finding a synthesis between them, leading to a complex, nuanced view of life's complexities.

For example, day and night appear to be opposites, yet their synthesis is noon and midnight. The fulcrum balance or halfway point between them is the synthesis of connectedness and separateness. Noon, afternoon, evening, late evening, night, midnight, after midnight, early morning, morning, day, late morning, and noon again—all have definite forms, light and dark, and every shade in between, but they are inseparably connected. Day follows night, and night follows day; you cannot have one without the other.

Similarly, we move from calm to excited and back to calm again; from waiting to arriving and waiting to receiving. An answer can change from no to yes or yes to no in a single moment. Yet, focusing only on the yes or the no misses all the moments connected and involved in the process of going from yes to no or no to yes.

Dialectics recognizes that everything changes, everything is a process, and everything is interconnected. This is true of every relationship in our lives, every circumstance, and every moment as it leads to the next. The only singular is the single moment, the now. Everything else is dialectic—a series of single moments. The dialectic is the process.

There are several ways to think about the dialectic as "both-and" rather than "either-or" or "this-or-that." It is helpful to consider the dialectic as a synthesis between seeming opposites. "Seeming" because of the recognition of interconnectedness rather than the separateness that is the reality of the world we live in.

The interconnectedness inherent in the dialectic recognizes the complex whole that emerges when we connect the constituent moments or parts. It is the reconciliation of the mutually contradictory thesis and antithesis that brings us to a broader truth, which is the synthesis. The synthesis is the balance of two seemingly opposing ideas: you and me, me and you, mine and yours, sadness and happiness, day and night, can and cannot, traveling to arriving, struggling and effective.

Dialectical Assumptions

All points of view have aspects that are both true and false within them.

Cause and effect is a rule of the universe.

Doing something and doing nothing are both responses.

Each moment is singular; together, they form a dialectic.

Human life includes both comfortable and uncomfortable experiences: ease and strife, happiness and sadness, hope and discouragement, easy days and hard days, good days and bad days.

Living life results in aging, and we can continue to live as we age.

Something can 'feel wrong' and still be a skillful choice.

There is always more than one true opinion, idea, desire, thought, or dream.

There is always more than one way to see a situation.

Two things that seem like or are opposites can both be true.

You are doing the best that you can, and you need to try harder, do better, and be more motivated to change.

You can accept the moment and still desire change.

You can accept yourself as you strive to improve yourself.

You can be right, and the other person can be right also.

You can take care of yourself and still allow for help or support from others.

Dialectic Examples

ability ∞ inability

above ∞ below

accept ∞ refuse

acquire ∞ lose

admire ∞ despise

affronted ∞ in different

aggravated ∞ calm

agree ∞ disagree

alert ∞ at rest

alone ∞ together

ancient ∞ modern

angry ∞ calm

annoyed ∞ relaxed

arrive ∞ leave

attend ∞ ignore

autopilot ∞ intention

balance ∞ imbalance

big ∞ small

blunt ∞ sharp

bold ∞ timid

boundary ∞ closeness

boundary ∞ connected

bright ∞ dim

broad ∞ narrow

buy ∞ sell

care ∞ neglect

chagrined ∞ relaxed

chaos ∞ order

childhood ∞ adulthood

choice ∞ force

civilized ∞ barbaric

clean ∞ dirty

cold ∞ hot

confess ∞ deny

confusion ∞ understanding

cruel ∞ kind

dangerous ∞ safe

dark ∞ bright

day ∞ night

deny ∞ accept

dialectic ∞ singular

difficult ∞ easy

disgruntled ∞ satisfied

displeased ∞ pleased

divine ∞ profane

domestic ∞ wild

early ∞ late

earn ∞ spend

east ∞ west

empty ∞ full

exasperated ∞ relaxed

false ∞ true

fat ∞ thin

fear ∞ courage

fine ∞ coarse

flexible ∞ inflexible

focus ∞ distraction

foolish ∞ wise

forward ∞ backward

freedom ∞ captivity

fresh ∞ stale

gain ∞ loss

general ∞ particular

gentle ∞ rough

give ∞ take

good ∞ bad

guilty ∞ innocent

happy ∞ sad

here ∞ there

high ∞ low

honor ∞ dishonor

huffy ∞ relaxed

humble ∞ proud

in ∞ out

include ∞ reject

independence ∞ autonomy

insulated ∞ exposed

irritated ∞ calm

joy ∞ sorrow

junior ∞ senior

just ∞ unjust

kind ∞ cruel

knowledge ∞ ignorance

laugh ∞ cry

lie ∞ truth

little ∞ much

lost ∞ found

love ∞ hate

majority ∞ minority

make ∞ break

masculine ∞ feminine

maximum ∞ minimum

mindless ∞ mindful

moral ∞ immoral

natural ∞ artificial

never ∞ always

night ∞ day

noise ∞ silence

north ∞ south

novice ∞ expert

offended ∞ pleased

one ∞ all

optimist ∞ pessimist

part ∞ whole	rich ∞ poor	superior ∞ inferior
permanent ∞ temporary	riled ∞ calm	sympathetic ∞ discord
personal ∞ professional	rough ∞ smooth	this ∞ that
pregnancy ∞ birth	savage ∞ kind	thought ∞ emotion
present ∞ absent	separate ∞ together	tight ∞ loose
pride ∞ humility	sharp ∞ dull	up ∞ down
problem ∞ solution	smile ∞ frown	victory ∞ defeat
profit ∞ loss	soft ∞ hard	weak ∞ strong
quick ∞ slow	solitude ∞ isolation	wisdom ∞ folly
receive ∞ give	solitude ∞ loneliness	wrong ∞ right
reject ∞ accept	stand ∞ sit	yes ∞ no
remember ∞ forget	stop ∞ start	youth ∞ aged

What impact might intentionally practice more dialectical thinking have on your life? How could your daily experiences change? Would adopting a more dialectical approach help you overcome ingrained, early-learned problematic responses?

Being Dialectic

Practice making informed compromises between all options based on rational analysis and respect for your emotional experience.

Avoid assumptions and blaming.

Embrace 'both' rather than 'either/or' thinking.

Be more flexible and approachable, and give the benefit of the doubt.

Dislike change but embrace it as inevitable.

Find ways to validate other people's experiences and perspectives.

Get unstuck from standoffs and conflicts, faultfinding, and blame.

Let go of black-and-white, all-or-nothing ways of thinking and experiencing.

Release superiority perspectives.

Let go of rigid expectations for others and from others.

Abandon self-righteous indignation.

Look for what is missing in your understanding and conclusions.

Notice the 'Buts'

Mindfulness of 'buts' is crucial because they can block flexible thinking. Here are some key points to consider:

Observe Your Patterns: Pay attention to how often you use 'but' in your thoughts and expressions. This can signal a rejection of part of the information rather than synthesizing it into the whole.

Power of 'But': 'But' is a powerful word that often disregards what came before it, signaling invalidation or uselessness. This type of black-and-white thinking opposes dialectical balance.

Goal of Dialectical Balance: Aim to synthesize the whole picture. By focusing on how often you use 'but,' you can start to change the pattern from 'but' to 'and.'

Example:

Expression: "I want to change jobs. I do not know how much longer I can keep working these kinds of shifts."

Response: "But, that would put a huge hole in our budget. No one else will pay you what you are making now."

Consider the Impact: Is this response balanced, supportive, and validating?

Revised Response: "I understand how hard this job has been on you, and I want you to know how much we appreciate how hard you are working. What are you thinking?"

Consider the Impact: Is this response balanced, supportive, and validating?

Practice 'And' Instead of 'But': This can increase your cognitive, emotional, and relational flexibility.

Would you like any further adjustments or additional examples?

2 Skill Areas

Dialectical Behavior Therapy (DBT) offers a wide range of useful skills that need to be understood, learned, tried, refined, and practiced in daily life. Each individual is different, and how each person effectively uses a skill will naturally vary. Many classical DBT skills are easily accessible on the internet, so I will not cover them here. Keep in mind that you may not need every skill.

Focus your skill development on areas of need or on refining existing skills to make them more effective or generalizable to a greater variety of situations and environments. Mindfulness is the exception. I have yet to meet a single individual, regardless of existing skills, who does not benefit from increased mindfulness skill development.

Mindfulness

Mindfulness skills form the foundation of all other skills. At its core, mindfulness is about living in the present moment. Without the ability to attend to, notice, and observe the moment, articulate your experience, and synthesize rational and emotional mind to participate in the moment, other skills are less effective at creating meaningful change.

Mindfulness skills include:

Mindful 'What' skills: Observing, describing, and participating.

Mindful 'How' skills: Practicing non-judgment, being one-mindful, and acting effectively. These skills involve the synthesis of reasonable mind and emotional mind, which enhances self-regulation and executive self-management.

Emotional Regulation

Emotional regulation is the ability to internally manage, initiate, modulate, or inhibit one's emotional states in a way that validates the relationship with oneself and is productive in meeting the challenges of the moment, skillfully in the long term.

Emotion regulation skills are critical and focus on the what, why, and how of emotions, as well as the initiation, proportional modulation, and inhibition of emotional states and reactions. It often surprises people to realize that, because the brain processes emotion and we are the bosses of our brains, we can learn to think in ways that help us feel more like we prefer to feel more often.

Distress Tolerance

Distress tolerance is the DBT term for managing discomfort. Tolerating distress is a critical life skill. Without it, life is not just difficult or painful—it is excruciating! Acceptance and tolerance of the normal, natural discomfort that accompanies reality are essential for making the best of non-preferred situations and not making problems worse.

Too often, we focus on avoiding life's pain, changing difficult situations, or spending huge amounts of our limited energy ignoring and suppressing the things that cause us discomfort. In DBT, we focus on dealing with the pain that is inevitable to our human condition by addressing it as it is. We take suffering and allow it to be painful. Pain can be managed by feeling it, dealing with it, and caring for it, which allows the pain to heal and improve.

Relationship Effectiveness

Relationship effectiveness is a two-fold skill. It involves building and maintaining a kind, gentle, loving relationship with oneself, as well as fostering kind, gentle, genuine, respectful, secure, and fulfilling relationships with others. These relationships should align with our personal values and vary in degrees of intimacy as appropriate. Relational connectedness is critical to long-term well-being and health.

These skills help us function effectively when trying to change something, such as making a request or setting healthy boundaries, like declining a request. The ultimate goal is to aid us in effectively meeting our needs and goals while living our values, fully embracing our identity with self-respect, and maintaining high-quality, long-lasting relationships.

Circle the skill areas you think would be useful for you to work on:

Mindfulness

Emotional Regulation

Distress Tolerance

Relationship Effectiveness

The goal of using skills is always to be effective. When we solve our problems without creating new ones, our lives improve. This requires us to consistently balance change and acceptance critically.

Take a few moments to jot down your thoughts about any work you think you need to do in these areas. What, if anything, do these topics bring up for you? Begin practicing metacognition—thinking about your thinking. What are your thoughts?

Journal

Change and Acceptance, A Mindful Dialectical Dance

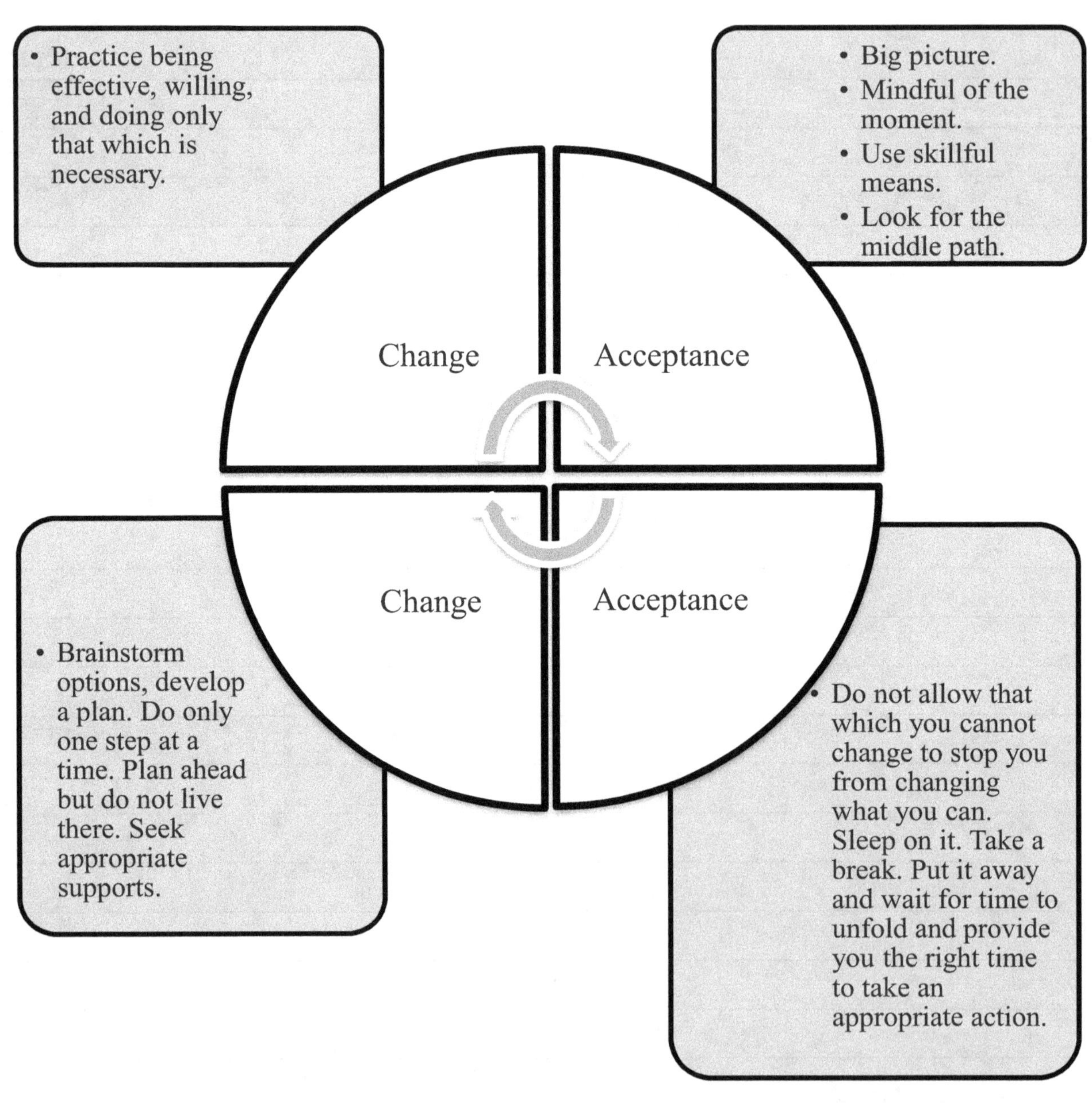

3 DBT Assumptions Expanded

DBT assumptions are hypotheses that we believe to be true and hold to be valid. The first five assumptions come directly from skills training manuals (Linehan, 1993; Linehan, 2014). The remainder I have developed to support nonjudgmental clear thinking in Wise Mind.

I am doing the best I can, and so are you.

I am doing the best I can, and so are you, but we need to do better, try harder, and be more motivated to change what is not working and is changeable.

I want to improve.

I may not have caused all my problems, but if I want them fixed, I must solve them anyway.

My current life experience is painful at times.

I understand that neither I nor anyone else can do what they do not know how to do.

I understand I must learn new behaviors to deal with the painful parts of my life in more skillful and effective ways.

I understand that there are many limitations related to this human life.

I understand that there is always a behavior I can practice to improve the quality of my life, relationships, and functioning.

I understand that change and acceptance are both difficult and, at times, feel wrong, bad, and unnatural. I understand that feeling wrong, bad, and unnatural does not mean they are bad, wrong, or unnatural.

I understand there is no absolute truth beyond the rules of the universe.

I understand that life is experienced from a point of view.

I understand that there is universal inherent value in humans and other living beings.

I understand that I must practice taking things in a well-meaning way if I am going to improve my relationships with others.

I understand that I must practice treating everyone, including myself, with more loving-kindness and compassion.

I understand that I must not act in ways that violate my values.

I understand that I must allow others to act in ways that align with their values.

I understand that judging is not my responsibility.

I understand that deep, genuine relationships with others require that I express my perspective, values, and preferences in a genuine, kind, and respectful way.

I understand that anything that needs to be said can be said with kindness and calm.

I understand that truth and facts are not weapons.

I understand that I must be willing to accept the discomfort of setting boundaries with others if others are to know what my boundaries are.

I understand that I must practice saying 'no' at times so I can say 'yes' to myself.

I understand that other people will not always agree with me, and that is all right.

I understand there are things I can change and things I cannot.

I understand if I spend my time and energy focused on things I cannot change, I will not have energy left to change the things that I could change.

I understand that the rules of the universe apply to everyone equally because the universe cannot violate its own rules.

4 Acceptance

Many of us mistakenly believe that if we experience discomfort in our lives, we must do something about it. We come to see being uncomfortable as unacceptable, leading us to go to great lengths to avoid it. The problem is that these efforts to avoid discomfort often make our painful problems worse, sometimes significantly so.

Radical acceptance requires us to let go of the idea of changing everything in our lives that is uncomfortable because some discomforts are unchangeable. Life, by its very nature, involves a certain amount of discomfort, challenge, and pain.

Think about a little one learning to walk. They don't just get up and walk down to the corner store for a candy bar. First, they hold their heads up and begin to look around; they must gain strength over time. They gain muscle control, hold their heads up while lying on their tummies, learn to sit up, reach for things, build muscle strength and balance, focus, and pull up. And, of course, they fall repeatedly. They get frustrated when they want something that is out of reach. This frustration drives them to keep trying. They don't think, "Well, I've been at this for a while now and I'm just not getting it. I guess I'll give up." Of course, they don't. If we did, none of us would be walking.

There are many parts of life that require us to accept the discomfort that comes with it, yet at times, we refuse. This refusal to accept that life changes are normal, and with these changes come challenges and discomfort, is problematic.

The fact is, discomfort is a fact. It just is, and the only way through is to acknowledge it, experience it, and allow its natural place in your life without trying to change it when it is unchangeable.

Radical acceptance means completely accepting discomfort as a normal and natural part of life. It is about accepting joy and discomfort. It is accepting each moment with its beginning, middle, and end.

We often think of radical acceptance as simply acceptance, but realistically, acceptance often leads to problem-solving. Accepting the moment does not mean we accept any ridiculous or horrible thing. It does not mean approving of the mistreatment of others or ourselves. Once you accept the truth that mistreatment is happening, it requires you to make an effort to stop it. Mistreatment continues because we do not accept that it is happening. We avoid it, turn away, blame, justify, or pretend we do not see or know. Acceptance leads to effectiveness, and effectiveness is focusing on what works.

Mindfulness is the practice of acceptance. It is the way of living with your mind wide open. It is very difficult to accept reality with your mind closed. If you are going to accept what is happening to you, to others, in your life, and in the world, your mind must be open to that reality. The basic idea of mindfulness is that awareness will set you free, mainly because you are completely aware in the present moment.

Mindfulness is not a place. You cannot travel there. Mindfulness is the journey. The journey to mindfulness is the practice, and the journey to mindfulness is mindfulness itself. It is the walking, the breathing, the focusing, the living in the moment, moment by moment, in each moment, and then in the next moment when you get there.

Choice

Acceptance of reality as it is, is an intentional choice. It is like coming to a fork in the road where you have to turn your mind towards 'Acceptance Road' and away from 'Rejecting Reality Road.'

Acceptance requires an inner commitment. Even so, the commitment itself is not acceptance; it simply turns you towards the path of acceptance. To be effective in acceptance, you must practice turning your mind and commitment to acceptance over and over, repeatedly, sometimes many times within just a few moments.

It is natural to want to turn away from and avoid pain in our lives and turn back towards comfort. We are comfort-driven by nature; it helps us survive. Pain avoidance is an automatic reflex, like pulling your hand away from a hot handle. However, emotional and psychological pain is not like physical pain. Accepting painful emotional and psychological realities requires mental effort and commitment. Turning the mind is a choice, a decision to not give up and turn toward comfort or denial. Turning the mind is a willing effort to deal with the painful emotional and psychological realities of life without avoidance or denial, holding on or holding away.

The remedy for suffering is a commitment to acceptance over and over, repeatedly, as long as it takes to ameliorate the pain and move towards healing. Acceptance is possible, and it will change your life.

Commitment is a dedication to a purpose. Commitment binds you to the direction of your intention, to a course of action. Whatever you practice, you will get better at. Commitment to behave in a particular way, a task, or a skill is directly related to the future performance of that way, task, or skill. Committed people are willing to keep to the task, focus on the job, or practice the skill.

Acceptance is acknowledging what is as it is; nothing more, nothing less. Acceptance is not approval. Acceptance is not a preference. To accept something is not the same as judging it good or bad, right or wrong, wanted or unwanted. Pain leads to suffering only when we refuse to accept that the pain exists. Acceptance is the only way through suffering.

Acceptance must be renewed. Once we find a way to move from non-acceptance, refusal, and denial of suffering, the immutable pain that is suffering begins to change. It is in this change that suffering becomes pain. Pain is mutable. We can feel it as it ebbs and flows. We can sit with it, feel it, and comfort it. Hold space for it and allow it to be what it is. It is this act of allowing yourself to be in the moment with pain as it is, a part of your reality, that allows the pain to be accepted. In that acceptance, as the moments unfold, it can change.

Freedom from suffering requires that we go deep within ourselves and accept that it is as it is. We must let ourselves completely stop fighting reality and take it completely as it is, adding nothing and holding nothing away. Feel it, truly feel it. Choosing to feel, allow, and accept it cannot change that it exists because it is what it is, and the time for it to have happened differently has passed. It is reality. Only then can it begin to heal, change, and allow us to move on.

How do you struggle with acceptance?

Denial

Pain happens; it is a normal necessary part of living. Pain is useful information such as when you touch a hot handle and you quickly move your hand to avoid a burn. If we were without the sensation of pain, we would be in serious trouble as a species. Pain in life cannot be avoided.

It is hard to accept many things that happen, the way a loved one died; the someone has treated you that you feel is unfair or unjust. The mind does not want to allow painful thoughts into consciousness so it will seek to avoid or alter these things.

When avoidance or alteration of painful thoughts becomes habitual, this behavior can turn into denial or other thinking errors. Denial seeks to keep us from conscious awareness of the pain. The irony is that the denial does not decrease pain; it perpetuates it, incubating it for a later time. Allowing it to grow and fester, seep into other areas of our lives. Poison our relationships with ourselves and others. It turns into suffering. Much like a thorn stuck in your finger and ignored swells and festers.

Write about a time when you accepted a reality you did not prefer and skillfully managed the challenge despite adversity. What was your triumph?

Suffering

Suffering sneaks up on us in many forms. Sometimes, we discount it and convince ourselves—or try to convince ourselves—that it does not matter, when in fact, it really does. Sometimes, we take a passive role or a victim stance, asking the universe or a higher power, "Why me?" and focusing on how badly we feel instead of what needs to be done to deal with the situation.

At times, it manifests as righteous anger: "That is not right… That is not fair… I cannot believe that happened…" Sometimes, we are stuck in the past, focusing on perceived injustices rather than the reality of the moment. Alternatively, worry can lead us to exhaustion and leave us stuck in passivity: "Oh my, oh my, oh my. I hope that does not happen." "I will not be able to deal with it." or "I cannot stand it."

These traps leave us vulnerable. The pain can be almost unbearable, but suffering is different. It's like having your foot caught in a bear trap with everything out of reach. The suffering becomes static, suspended, or held away, and the pain becomes immutable—a constant companion.

When we refuse to accept the pain, we suffer. When we cling to getting what we want and refuse to accept what we have, we suffer. When we fight reality, oppose the inevitable, and struggle against what is, we suffer. It is inevitable. Non-acceptance of pain is suffering.

It is the denial, avoidance, and rejection of pain that leads to our suffering. Denial does not decrease pain; it multiplies it exponentially, allowing it to seep insidiously into other areas of our lives. No living being can deal with any problem that they do not or will not acknowledge exists. Non-acceptance diminishes opportunities for changing things that are changeable because the energy that might otherwise be available to change things is being utilized to deny, distort, or avoid reality.

Acceptance is the commitment to accept life as it is, in all of its shades, lessons, and opportunities. Acceptance allows us to see the lessons and the blessings, to feel, learn, and thrive despite life's challenges. It helps us understand that life's challenges are part of the pattern and tapestry of our lives. None of us knows where we are going or why we are here. How could we? Our view is too limited.

Often, the painful lessons of today lead to our growth tomorrow. Think of running downhill. If you or I run downhill fast enough, we will fall on our face. We must because gravity works equally for everyone on this planet. Think of falling as a lesson in gravity. It would be highly ineffective to curse the ground for gravity because, without gravity, the rules of nature would not work on this planet. We would have no atmosphere to breathe, so there would be no life and no running. Acceptance of all the rules of the world as they are is the key to freedom— not from the pain that is life, but from suffering.

The dialectic is that we experience our existence in the universe personally, so much so that we take things personally when they are not about us. The universe, to a great degree, is impersonal, but we experience it personally. So, when unpreferred things happen "to" us, we conclude that it is about us. Often, this is not the case. The universe works the way it works, and we are fundamentally bound by those rules. To be at a place in time where something occurs, someone does something to someone else, to be a child in a household or an employee working a job—things happen because someone chose to do them, not necessarily because someone chose to do them to us. Oftentimes, we are just the other party involved because we are there, not by design.

Even if it is by design, we are not responsible for the behaviors or choices of others. Their choices and behaviors are about them and their state of mind, not about us. Accepting and acknowledging that it "feels" like it is about us, then working through that emotional or somatic experience, is acceptance. Acceptance is the path to freedom from the pain of the experience.

Contemplate the ways you may be suffering today. What thoughts, emotions, sensations in your body, or behavior patterns may be related to this suffering?

Should

We often add "should" to reality. Reality "should" be different, but the universe simply follows its own rules. It does not adhere to our ideas of what we think reality should be. Whatever occurs in the universe follows these rules. The universe cannot break its own rules. It would be like gravity working differently for you than it does for me. That simply cannot happen in this universe, on this planet, at this time, without extreme scientific intervention. Therefore, whatever happens should happen. It must happen because each moment before led to it.

This does not mean that we want things to happen this way or that way. It does not mean that we prefer or like what is or has happened. And it certainly does not mean we will not work to change things. It simply means that everything that happens has a cause. There is a cause and then an effect. Whatever happens cannot be different unless a new cause arises to make it occur differently.

"Shoulds" are a trap. They are a wish for the effect to be different, for the world to be different, for the universe to operate differently than it does. It is a magical wish to change the rules of the universe. The universe simply cannot be different than it is. Time, cause and effect, gravity, momentum, quantum states—all must be exactly as they are. It is from this understanding that we must start if we are to be more skillful in creating causes that lead to more preferred effects, when possible. If there is a cause, there will be a result, whether we agree with this fact or not. It exists and will continue to exist as long as the rules of the universe act upon us on this planet as they do. We must conclude and accept that everything at this moment is as it should be because of each moment that came before, the previous moment, this moment, and soon the next moment.

Of course, this is only true until some cause changes, and then the effect must change too. Sometimes in ways that are anticipated and predictable, but also at times in ways that are unanticipated and unpredictable. Everything in the universe being as it should be is fundamental to acceptance. Accepting this moment as it is, in this moment, is a fact.

How do you think "shoulds" are a problem for you?

5 Wise Mind

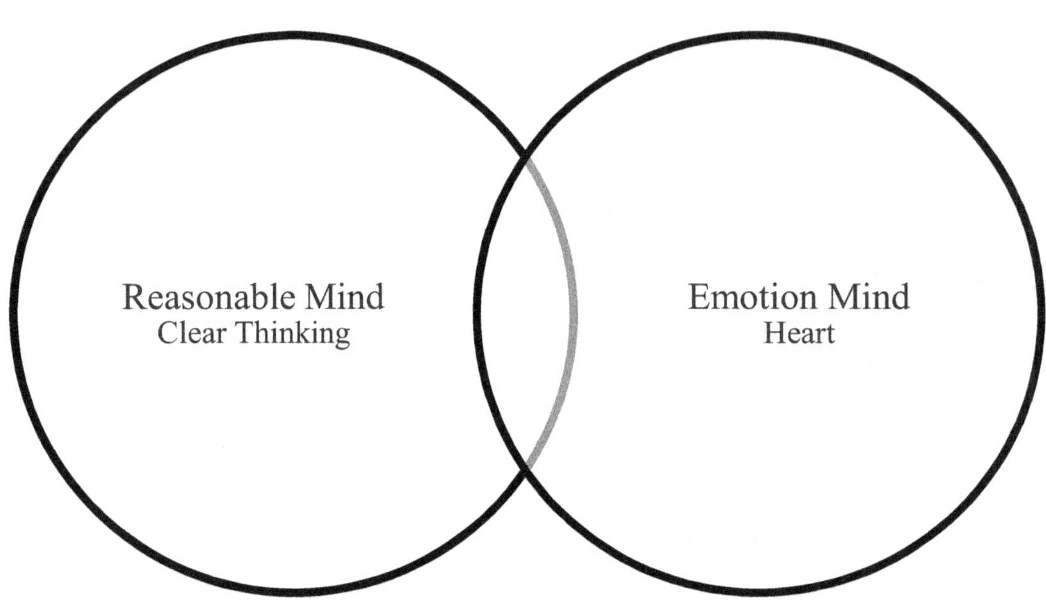

Wise Mind

Middle Ground

Dialectic Balance

Mindfulness is...

Attending and Observing: attending to the current moment as each new moment comes into being as it is the intention of attention without judgment.

Being, Seeing and Feeling the Moment: to intentionally, nonjudgmentally be your whole self in the moment, see the moment and feel the moment as it is.

Choiceless Awareness: to intentionally allow what is to be, to be; to be radically non-reactively present in awareness without preference, effort to hold on to or change the moment.

Focused, Unfocused Attention: intentional soft attentional focus of noticing how the mind moves from thought to thought, like clouds as they pass in the sky, observing and noticing without holding on or pushing away.

One In The Moment: the practice of intentionally, nonjudgmentally observing, describing and participating within the present moment.

Open Monitoring: the intentional awareness of thoughts, emotions, and sensations without attachment to them.

Nonjudgmentally: mindful observing and noticing, with intention, without judging, or ego attachment.

Practice Makes Permanent: anything you practice you become better at. Practice changes the brain.

Soft Spacious Mind: the practice of intentionally bringing awareness to the experience of the present moment with curiosity, gentleness, kindness, and acceptance.

Mindfulness is a skill that can be cultivated. Aim for a minimum of five minutes of mindfulness daily. Many excellent guided mindfulness activities are available free on YouTube.

Consider these aspects of mindfulness. Which appeal to you most? Why?

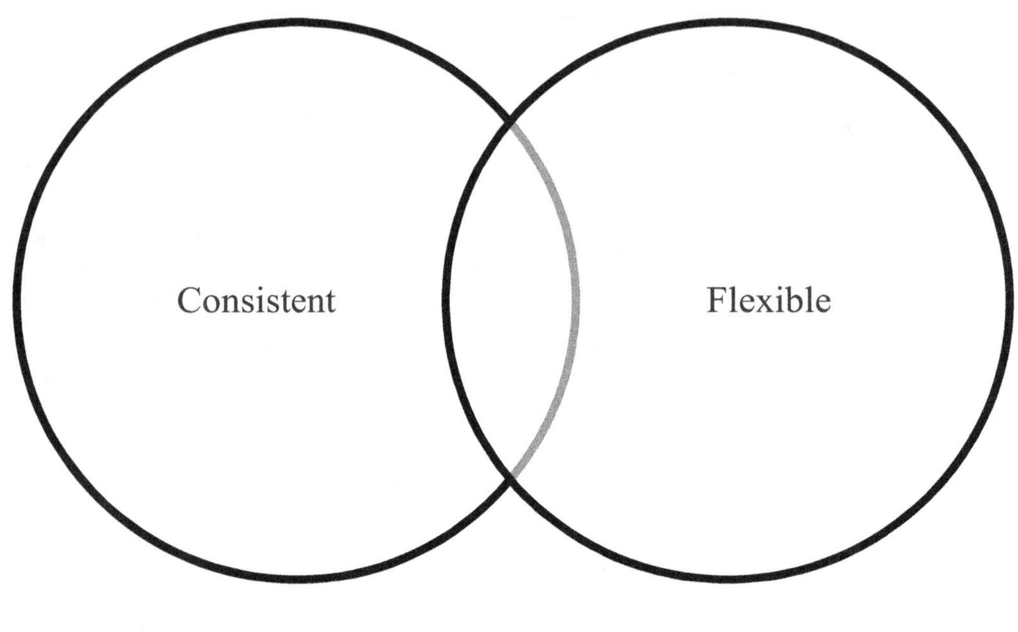

Clear Thinking

Stable, Reasonable & Logical   Able to Respond to Circumstances

How many things in your life can you think of that it would benefit you to be more stable, reasonable, logical and flexible?

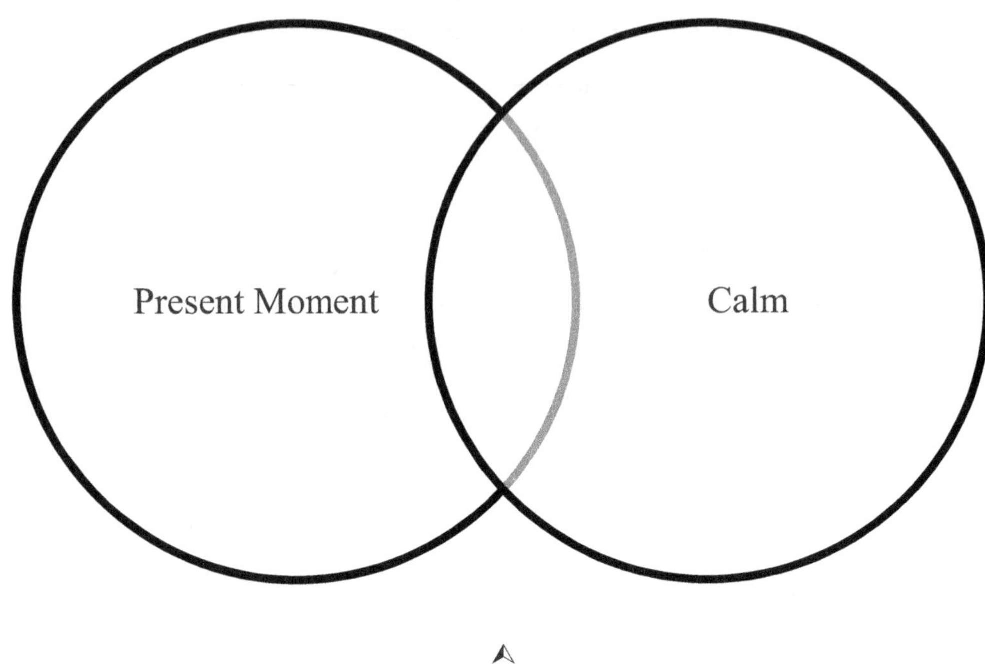

Bed Mindfulness

Mindfulness is paying attention in a particular way, nonjudgmentally, at the moment.

By practicing cultivating calm in your mind to only allow the experience of the moment to engulf and hold you. Bed mindfulness is such mindfulness.

After you get into bed, if you are like most people the events, random thoughts and concerns of the day rush in upon you now that the external noise of your environment is quiet.

Bedtime is not a problem-solving opportunity; it is an opportunity to rest for the body and mind.

Before bedtime:

- Spend some time in the quiet at a time of the afternoon or early evening, allow your thoughts to float in and out of your awareness, allow your wise minded deep knowing to provide you solutions to the struggles you experience. Ask your wise mind for guidance.

- Keep a gratitude journal.

- Keep a concerns and solutions journal.

- Practice only considering problems at a place and time that you might have an actual opportunity to address them skillfully and effectively. This is not while in bed.

By taking control of your mind you are becoming master of your time and attention. Your mind will learn to follow your guidance and not just go wherever, whenever it wants. Just like your feet. This does require practice, so be patient.

<u>Bedtime Breathing, One in the Moment</u>

Breath Mindfulness. Slow the heart rate and soothe the body into a restful sleep.

Inhale, while thinking 'in'.

Exhale, while thinking 'out'.

Repeat.

If you find your mind drifting from your breath just notice it, acknowledge it without judgment and bring your attention back to your breath.

You will hear and feel your heart rate slow down, and your mind quiet as your whole body relaxes. Keep focusing on your breath until you fall asleep.

Inhale
Exhale
One in
the
Moment

Infinite to Finite

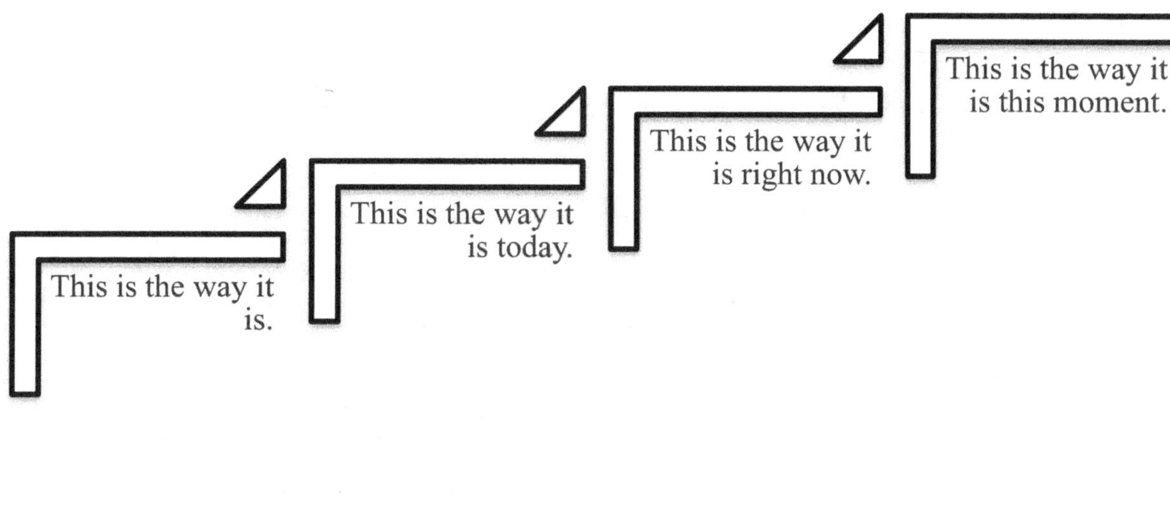

Can you identify any ways you can increase your flexible thinking through the use of infinite to finite?

Universe Cannot Break Its Own Rules

The universe cannot break its own rules.

Therefore, whatever happens, should happen, must happen.

As a result of each moment that came before.

Everything that happens has been caused, because time runs one direction, from the past to now to the future.

Since the cause cannot now be different.

This moment is what it is.

It is because it must be.

Your choice is what to do with it now.

FOOD for the Soul

FOOD for the Soul is a validation skill focused upon mindful validation.

F   Focus on the inherent worth of the person, whether it is yourself or someone else. Find what is true or valid about the experience, without thinking that you have to agree or approve. Find what makes sense. Validate that.

O   Observe by listening carefully to what is being said with words, expressions, body language. State the unstated by noting what is not being said. Seek verification of inferences. Ask to understand.

O   One the moment. Hold space or time when needed. Do not multitask.

D   Describe the facts of the situation nonjudgmentally; specifically, accurately and proportionally.

Validating yourself is as important as validating others. Validation is the basis of unconditional positive regard and acceptance of the human condition that we all share.

Remember that when validating yourself that even if you realize that the thoughts you are having are irrational or based upon a thinking error is important to understand and validate that they exist and you feel them, sometimes strongly, at the moment.

If you are validating others, even if you disagree with their behavior, find something you can empathize with and connect with.

How can you use this skill to increase validation in your relationships? Can you think of any times in the past you could have validated more and perhaps changed an outcome?

Mindfulness Balance

Goal: Balance the mind and calm the body.

Choose a focal point several feet in front of you. Keep your eyes focused on that point while you slightly lift the weight off one foot and shift it to the other.

Stand gently on one foot; holding the back of a chair for balance, if you need to.

Maintain awareness of yourself in your situation, think 'balance' or 'calm' gently to yourself.

Focus on bring calm awareness of the moment to yourself.

Breathe normally, feeling each breath in your body as you focus on balancing and calming yourself at the moment. Repeat on the other foot.

References

Houts, L. (2022). CBT - DBT Companion for Everyday: Skills, Worksheets & Direct
Clinical Practice Resources. Independently published.

Linehan, M. (1993). Cognitive-behavioral treatment of borderline personality disorder.
Guilford Press.

Linehan, M. (n.d.). DBT? Skills training manual (1st ed.). Guilford Publications.

Linehan, M. M. (2014). DBT skills training handouts and worksheets (2nd ed.). Guilford
Publications.

www.ingramcontent.com/pod-product-compliance
Lightning Source LLC
Chambersburg PA
CBHW081456250726
48662CB00009B/3112